D0853976

JUNIOR
BIOGRAPHY
FROM
ANCIENT
CIVILIZATIONS

ALEXANDER
THE GREAT

JOHN BANKSTON

Mitchell Lane
PUBLISHERS

P.O. Box 196
Hockessin, Delaware 19707
Visit us on the web (www.mitchelllane.com
Comments? Email us (mitchelllane@mitchelllane.com

JUNIOR BIOGRAPHY FROM ANCIENT CIVILIZATIONS

Alexander the Great • Archimedes
Augustus Caesar • Confucius • Genghis Khan
Homer • Leif Erikson • Marco Polo
Nero • Socrates

ABOUT THE AUTHOR (Born in Boston, Massachusetts, John Bankston began writing articles while still a teenager. Since then, over two hundred of his articles have been published in magazines and newspapers across the country, including travel articles in *The Tallahassee Democrat, The Orlando Sentinel* and *The Tallahassean.* He is the author of over eighty books for young adults, including biographies of scientist Stephen Hawking, author F. Scott Fitzgerald and actor Jodi Foster.

Because Alexander the Great lived over two thousand years ago, sources of information are sometimes incomplete or inconsistent. In some instances, the author has described what might have happened in order to add interest and intrigue appropriate for the age level of the reader.

Printing 1 2 3 4 5 6 7 8 9

**Library of Congress
Cataloging-in-Publication Data**
Bankston, John, 1974–
 Alexander the Great / by John Bankston.
    pages cm. — (Junior biography from ancient civilizations
 Includes bibliographical references and index.
 ISBN 978-1-61228-431-6 (library bound
 1. Alexander, the Great, 356 B.C.–323 B.C.—
Juvenile literature. 2. Greece—History—
Macedonian Expansion, 359–323 B.C.—Juvenile
literature. 3. Generals—Greece—Biography—
Juvenile literature. 4. Greece—Kings and
rulers—Biography—Juvenile literature. I. Title.
DF234.B329 2013
938'.07092—dc23
[B]
                                                    2013012553
eBook ISBN: 9781612284934

PLB

CONTENTS

Phonetic pronunciations of words in **bold**
can be found on page 46.

Artwork often portrays Alexander the Great as a powerful soldier, like in this painting by Rembrandt. But before he was a leader, he was a boy filled with curiosity and eager to learn.

CHAPTER 1

A Bold Boy

The boy was not afraid of the men. They towered over him, speaking in gruff voices. The men were ambassadors—official representatives of the King of **Persia**.*

The boy was young—six or seven years old. Some his age are shy. They might try to hide. They don't like talking to adults they don't know. This boy was not like that. Instead, he started asking the men questions.

What was the road to Persia like?

How many soldiers did their king command?

What was the king like?

". . . the questions he asked them, which were far from being childish . . . that they were struck with admiration of him," one writer later wrote. In fact, they thought the boy was already bolder than his father.[1]

The bold boy was named Alexander. His father, Philip, was king. Alexander lived over 2,300 years ago, but he is still remembered today. New books are written about him every year. He became a great soldier, uniting Greece and winning battles across Asia.

*For pronunciations of words in **bold**, see page 46.

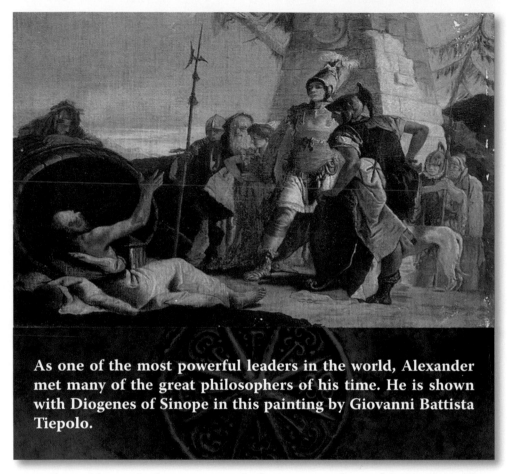

As one of the most powerful leaders in the world, Alexander met many of the great philosophers of his time. He is shown with Diogenes of Sinope in this painting by Giovanni Battista Tiepolo.

When Alexander's army invaded a country, his soldiers were often welcomed. In some places, the leaders forced the people to pay very high taxes. Money was taken from them for growing food or selling goods. In other countries, people could not pray to their god or build their own churches.

Sometimes after Alexander entered a country, he lowered the taxes. He let people worship whomever they wished and helped them build temples for their religion. He even learned about their religions.

Alexander was one of the greatest military leaders who ever lived. But in the beginning, he was just a little boy—a boy who was both bold and a little too smart for his own good.

Ancient Tales

Alexander lived thousands of years before video cameras and televisions. Stories were written about him hundreds of years before the printing press allowed books to be easily produced. So how do we know so much about him?

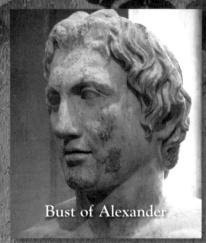

Bust of Alexander

Alexander was well known. As ruler of a larger empire, he was like today's movie stars. His adventures were written down by eyewitnesses— people who saw what he did. He hired a royal secretary who kept a journal. There was also a historian—the nephew of one of his teachers—who wrote about Alexander.

Several hundred years later, authors relied on this information to write books about his life. One of the best known is the Greek writer **Plutarch** of **Chaeronea**. He wrote his stories about Alexander at the end of the first century CE, about four hundred years after Alexander lived.

Archaeologists are scientists who study ancient people. Beginning in the 1800s, archaeologists unearthed ruins from **Macedonia** to India and **Afghanistan**. These relics helped prove some of the stories told about Alexander.

Still, the complete truth of Alexander's life is not known. Events were described in different ways by different eyewitnesses. It isn't always possible to know which story is true. Even his birthday is not known for certain. Still, there is much we can learn about Alexander from the words of those who knew him, and those who were inspired by his journey.

Before he was a teenager, Alexander's reputation was beginning to be formed. When no one else could tame the horse named Bucephalus, Alexander did just that.

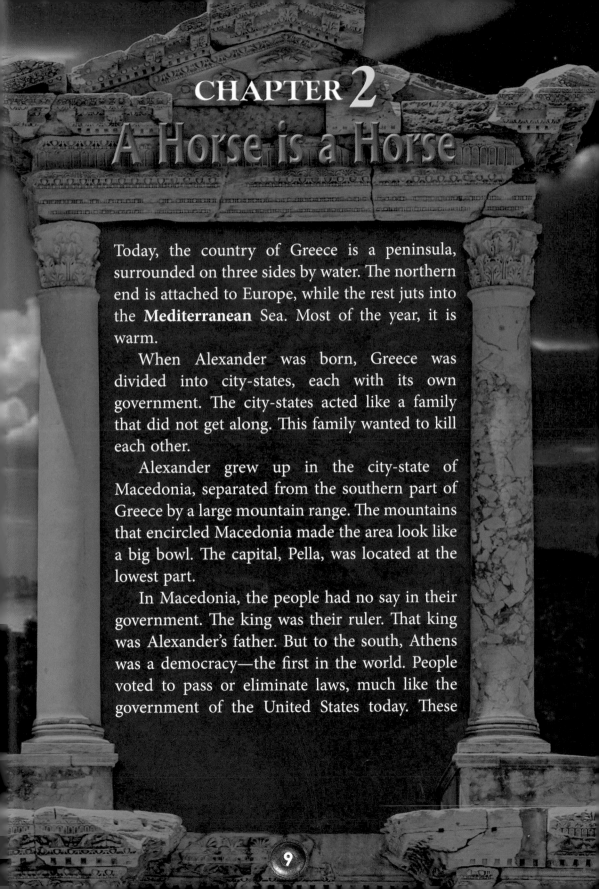

CHAPTER 2
A Horse is a Horse

Today, the country of Greece is a peninsula, surrounded on three sides by water. The northern end is attached to Europe, while the rest juts into the **Mediterranean** Sea. Most of the year, it is warm.

When Alexander was born, Greece was divided into city-states, each with its own government. The city-states acted like a family that did not get along. This family wanted to kill each other.

Alexander grew up in the city-state of Macedonia, separated from the southern part of Greece by a large mountain range. The mountains that encircled Macedonia made the area look like a big bowl. The capital, Pella, was located at the lowest part.

In Macedonia, the people had no say in their government. The king was their ruler. That king was Alexander's father. But to the south, Athens was a democracy—the first in the world. People voted to pass or eliminate laws, much like the government of the United States today. These differences in government caused many of the conflicts between the city-states.

People were farming in Greece over 8,000 years ago. The recorded history of Greek government begins in 1200 BCE. Today, the way doctors practice medicine, the way people vote, and even the Olympic Games all have their roots in ancient Greece.

Alexander's mother, **Olympias**, claimed to be related to Helen of Troy and **Achilles**. Her name was also connected to Greek myths.

Olympias was Philip's third wife. She was also his most difficult.

Olympias worshiped **Dionysus**, the god of good times. She used snakes in her prayers. She also kept them as pets and even slept with them. King Philip hated snakes.

In Macedonia, only men ruled. If Philip wanted his child to take over the throne, he needed a boy. It was a very good day when King Philip learned about Alexander's birth. On the same day, he had already won a major battle and his horse had won its race in the Olympics.

When Alexander was twelve years old, King Philip was looking to buy a horse. One of the horses that was offered to him was wild and unpredictable. The horse bucked and whinnied. Even the horse sellers admitted it was not the right one for his family. But Alexander disagreed. "What a horse they are losing, because, for lack of skill and courage, they cannot manage him!" he said.[1]

What good was a horse no one could ride? Riding a horse was much harder in those days. There were no stirrups for a rider's feet. The rider used his legs to grip the horse. At least horses were smaller—about the size of a large pony. It was easier to get on and hold on.

Alexander said he could ride the horse. His father laughed.

The historian Plutarch writes that, "Philip at first took no notice of what he said; but when he heard him repeat the same thing several times, and saw he was [upset] to see the horse sent away, [Philip said], 'Do you reproach those who are older than yourself, as if you knew more, and were better able to manage him than they?' "[2]

Alexander had no doubt. "I could manage this horse better than others do." If he could not ride the horse, he would pay for it. The horse cost a lot of money.[3]

But if Alexander could ride the horse, he wanted to keep it. King Philip agreed.

Alexander ran up to the animal. He spoke softly. He patted its head. And he realized something no one else had—the horse was afraid of its own shadow. Gently, Alexander took the horse's bridle. He turned it around, facing the sun. Then he got on.

The horse took off! It raced away in a cloud of dust. Alexander left behind a worried king and some very scared sellers. If their horse hurt the boy, they might be killed.

After a few minutes, Alexander returned, unhurt. The Greek writer Plutarch wrote:

". . . they all burst out into acclamations of applause; and his father shedding tears, it is said, for joy, kissed him as he came down from his horse, and . . . said, 'O my son, look thee out a kingdom equal to and worthy of thyself, for Macedonia is too little for thee.' "[4]

The horse was called Bucephalus, a Greek word meaning "ox head." It was named for being stubborn, but Alexander didn't mind. Bucephalus would be Alexander's horse for most of his life. He trusted it more than he trusted most men. He loved it more than his own father. Then again, the horse was more reliable.

This statue of Alexander's father, Philip II of Macedon, stands in Thessaloniki, Greece.

Alexander's life was more than riding horses. Someday he could be king. His father was worried he would not be ready.

Alexander is usually described as having very thick, curly hair. It may have been blonde when he was younger. As a man, he was not very tall, but he was in very good shape. His hair was dark brown when he was grown up. His eyes were two different colors. One was blue, the other was gray.

The Greeks believed the gods blessed good-looking people more than others. This is why the Greeks thought they made the best rulers. Alexander was considered gorgeous. He was also very spoiled.

Olympias wanted her son to be happy. She gave him gifts and made sure he had his favorite food. Young Alexander's life was easy. His father thought it was too easy. King Philip was too busy fighting battles to spend much time with Alexander. When he did, the king worried that his wife was turning their son into a weakling.

King Philip believed Alexander needed a strong man to teach him how to be a warrior. So he hired one.

Statue of Olympias and Alexander at Schönbrunn Palace in Vienna, Austria

Greece is a country of stories. These stories are called myths. Greek myths feature gods and goddesses, heroes and heroines. The king of the gods was **Zeus**; the goddess of love was **Aphrodite**.

Homer

Stories about ancient battles and their heroes were written by Homer around the eighth century BCE. Homer's book the *Iliad* describes the end of the Trojan War and the infamous Trojan Horse. The war had begun when Helen, the most beautiful woman in the world, was abducted from Greece and taken to Troy. After ten years of fighting, the Greeks still had not won Helen back. So they constructed a large wooden horse, left it outside the gates of Troy, and pretended to sail away. Believing it was a victory trophy, the Trojans brought it inside. It was actually filled with Greeks, who crept out at night and destroyed the city of Troy.

Alexander's mother told him he was related to Achilles. Achilles was the main hero of the Trojan War in Homer's *Iliad*. His mother dipped him in the River **Styx** as an infant, which was said to have protected him. Unfortunately, she held him by the heel, and this spot was unprotected. When he was injured there, he died. Today when people say someone has an "Achilles' heel," it means they have a weakness in a particular area.

A painting showing Alexander the Great dressed for battle. The son of a king, Alexander received the same brutal training as any soldier. This paid off when he was tested in battle.

CHAPTER 3
School of Hard Knocks

When Alexander was about eight years old, King Philip hired a tutor from Olympias's family to teach Alexander how to be a soldier.

King Philip expected his son to receive the best possible training. The tutor, named Leonidas, was not worried. He planned to tame Alexander just like the young prince had tamed Bucephalus. Except Alexander had been gentle.

King Philip wanted Leonidas to teach his son math along with how to use a bow and arrow. The tutor taught Alexander much more than that—he taught him to survive.

Until that point, Alexander had enjoyed good food, plenty of rest, and the best toys. **Leonidas** changed all that.

Being the King's son did not get Alexander special treatment. His tutor went through his things. When he found gifts from Olympias, Leonidas threw them away. He kept the boy from sleeping. He took away his food and his water. He trained him like the best fighters in the world.

Alexander may have hated the training. But a decade later, the lessons helped save his life. They also saved the lives of thousands of his soldiers.

Still, not every lesson took. One day, Alexander offered an enormous sacrifice of incense. His teacher was angry. Leonidas ". . . told him it became him to be more sparing in his offerings, and not be so profuse till he was master of the countries which those . . . spices came from."[1]

Years later, Alexander ruled over a kingdom. After a victory in battle, he sent his former teacher a huge amount of spices. "So Alexander now wrote to him, saying, 'We have sent you abundance of myrrh and frankincense, that for the future you may not be stingy to the gods.' "[2]

Although Leonidas took away Alexander's joy, his next tutor returned it. **Lysimachus** made up a game in which the prince pretended to be Achilles. This made his mother happy. After all, she believed her son and the Greek hero were related.

To Alexander, Lysimachus became like a father. His real one was usually not around. Philip had used the wealth from Macedonia's gold mines to train some of the best soldiers in Greece. But he didn't just send them off to battle—he joined them. His body was marked by the injuries he'd gotten fighting. He lost an eye in one battle and walked with a limp after his leg was cut in another.

Alexander might have felt like the only time King Philip dropped by was when he returned to give him a new tutor. By the time Alexander was a teenager, he was trained as a soldier. His next teacher would teach him how to be a king.

Military Tactics—The King Philip Fighting Style

Alexander is remembered as a great military leader. Much of what he learned about war, he learned from his dad. Indeed, his father was so successful that Alexander worried that by the time he became king, there would not be any more land to conquer!

Ancient battles were a free-for-all. Soldiers fought one-on-one, with little order or discipline. King Philip changed that. Under his command, soldiers fought in formation. They lined up and stayed lined up.

Bust of King Philip

King Philip is perhaps best remembered for inventing the **sarissa**, a fourteen-foot-long pole topped with a sharp blade. Soldiers with this weapon marched in a phalanx—a tight group of soldiers. It was considered almost unstoppable.

The Macedonian phalanx counter-attacks during the Battle of the Carts

Famous in his time and still well known in ours, Alexander the Great began his military training at a young age.

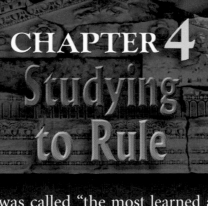

CHAPTER 4
Studying to Rule

Aristotle was called "the most learned and most celebrated philosopher of his time." He might have been the best teacher in the world. Still, Alexander probably laughed when they first met. The tutor was very skinny with tiny eyes. He dressed in wild clothes; on his fingers were crazy rings. His speech seemed odd.[1]

What Aristotle said, however, silenced the prince. The way he taught was different from the others. Alexander soon knew that Aristotle was very smart.

Aristotle's father was a royal doctor in Macedonia when Philip's own father was king. Philip was almost Aristotle's age. At seventeen, Aristotle left for a well-known school in Athens called the Academy, where he became a teacher. When the head teacher died, Aristotle left the school. He may have had a disagreement with the new head teacher. With a growing number of people in Athens who did not like Macedonians, it is also possible that Aristotle feared for his life. Then the king hired him.

Aristotle believed in learning by watching and doing. He studied tadpoles in a swamp. He made medicine from plants. Until Aristotle arrived, Alexander did not go to school. The school came to him. That changed as the prince entered his teens.

Aristotle set up a small school in **Mieza**, just west of Pella. Alexander was not his only student. Aristotle believed that people need each other. The sons of men who worked for Philip attended with Alexander. In those days, girls did not go to school.

Being the son of a king has its advantages—like being taught by one of the best teachers who ever lived. Here an engraving by Charles Laplante shows Aristotle teaching a teenage Alexander.

One of Alexander's classmates was **Ptolemy**, who would later rule Egypt. Another was **Cassander**, the son of Philip's General **Antipater**. Still, for the prince, his most important classmate was **Hephaestion**.

Hephaestion became his best friend. As a teenager, Alexander was not very interested in dating. Instead, he spent his time outside of school with Hephaestion.

Aristotle wrote books about government, science, and the arts. He believed the world was round. He decided whales were not fish (they aren't, they are mammals). Alexander's favorite classes were poetry, science, and medicine. "Alexander spent these school hours with one of the most tireless and wide-ranging minds which has ever lived," wrote one author.[2] Alexander learned how to cure a snakebite or poisoning. He studied how to make medicines from plants. Years later, those lessons helped him save the soldiers he fought with.

When Alexander was sixteen, his father decided to spend more time with him. King Philip did not take his son fishing or camping. He took him into battle.

Alexander's first test came not on the battlefield, but on the throne. King Philip left to fight a war. Before he did, he put Alexander in charge of the kingdom. He was sixteen years old.

It was around 340 BCE when the **Maedi** rebelled. With King Philip gone, they thought they could do as they pleased.

They were wrong.

As the Maedi attacked a village to the north of Pella, Alexander prepared. General Antipater helped the young prince select the best soldiers. Then he rode with them toward the rebelling Maedi.

Alexander's army attacked. They took over the Maedi's main village and killed most of the rebels. Then Alexander renamed the town. He called it Alexandropolis.

When King Philip returned, he was very proud. He was also worried. He wondered if his son wanted to keep the throne.

Two years later, he saw his son in action.

King Philip had united almost all of the city-states in Greece. Although he did not conquer Athens, Sparta, or Corinth, he brought them into the Corinthian League, and declared himself leader of this league.

Many of the people in Athens looked down on Macedonia. They saw Athens as the center of art and science, and thought most people who lived in Macedonia were shepherds who were even dumber than their sheep. Athenians hated being ruled by anyone, but especially a Macedonian.

In August of 338, they joined with the soldiers of Thebes, including the elite "Sacred Band." They did not know King Philip had a secret weapon.

Riding astride Bucephalus, eighteen-year-old Alexander led the cavalry—a special type of army made up of horses and the soldiers who ride them. When Alexander's cavalry attacked, it was brutal. His father dealt with the Athenians. Alexander took care of the Thebans.

Plutarch claimed, "At the battle of Chaeronea, which his father fought against the Grecians, [Alexander] is said to have been the first man that charged the Thebans' sacred band."[3] Thousands of Athenians and Thebans were killed, but the Sacred Band would not surrender. They kept fighting. Almost their entire force of three hundred men was killed.

In another battle, Alexander did not just win. He saved his father's life. During a fight, King Philip was surrounded. One attacker sliced his leg and he went to the ground. Alexander later said his father pretended to be dead while he fought off the attackers.

Alexander expected praise, but instead, his father treated him even worse. Maybe he was embarrassed that his son had saved him. Maybe the story wasn't true. Or maybe he just thought Alexander wanted to get rid of him so he could be king.

Growing tired of her temper and her snakes, King Philip stopped spending time with Alexander's mother, Olympias. He began seeing **Cleopatra**, the young niece of one of his generals.

Never say surrender! The Sacred Band of Thebes was well known for fighting to the death. After they met Alexander at the Battle of Chaeronea, there weren't many of them left.

Like many Greeks then, the king had more than one wife. Some stories say he had eight!

King Philip's wedding to Cleopatra was not a happy day for Alexander. He sat across from his father and joked that he would invite King Philip to Olympias's wedding. His father did not laugh.

Plutarch tells what happened next. "At the wedding of Cleopatra, whom Philip fell in love with and married, she being much too young for him, her uncle **Attalus** [made a toast] the Macedonians would implore the gods to give them a lawful successor to the kingdom by his niece."[4]

Asking that Cleopatra produce a son for the throne meant Attalus thought Alexander would not be king. Alexander was insulted and threw a cup at his head, calling Attalus a villain.

Plutarch wrote that, "Then Philip, taking Attalus's part, rose up and would have run his son through [with a sword]; but by good fortune for them both, either his over-hasty rage, or the wine he had drunk, made his foot slip, so that he fell down on the floor. At which Alexander reproachfully insulted over him ('See there,' said he, 'the man who makes preparations to pass out of Europe into Asia, overturned in passing from one seat to another.' ")[5]

Alexander stormed out. The next day, he left with his mother. He took Olympias to stay with her family in **Epirus**, then he traveled to **Illyria**.

A few months later, King Philip was visited by **Demaratus**, an old friend. When Philip asked about how the Greek city-states were getting along, Demaratus had another question. How could Philip be so concerned with peace in the country when he didn't have peace within his own family? Realizing that Demaratus was right, King Philip asked Alexander to come home.

By 336 BCE, Alexander and his father were getting along again. Alexander was back in Macedonia, attending his sister's wedding. She was marrying her uncle, also named Alexander. Relationships in ancient Greece can be confusing!

The day after the wedding, King Philip hosted a show. He entered the arena accompanied by the two Alexanders. When a royal bodyguard named **Pausanias** approached, no one was worried. Pausanias took out a short sword and stabbed King Philip.

The king died with Alexander by his side. Pausanias was caught and killed. That day, Alexander's life changed. He became the king, ruler over most of Greece. He was twenty years old.

For Aristotle, the subject connecting all other subjects was philosophy. From a Greek word meaning "the love of wisdom," philosophy has been described as the search for meaning in the universe. It is a way of thinking. Philosophers like Aristotle looked at the world and how people behaved in it. Philosophers would also study subjects like science and math.

Just as Alexander was Aristotle's student, Aristotle was a student of **Plato**. The founder of the Academy, the Athens

Plato and Aristotle in
The School of Athens
by Raphael

Socrates Teaching Perikles
by Nicolas Guibal

school where Aristotle learned and taught, Plato also wrote down the words of his own teacher, **Socrates**. Socrates developed a method of teaching that involved talking about a subject with students, often answering questions with questions. Called the **Socratic** method, it is still widely used in schools today.

When a powerful leader is killed, people often wonder if someone other than the actual killer is involved. This painting by André Castigne shows the assassination of Philip II, which some people thought was ordered by Alexander.

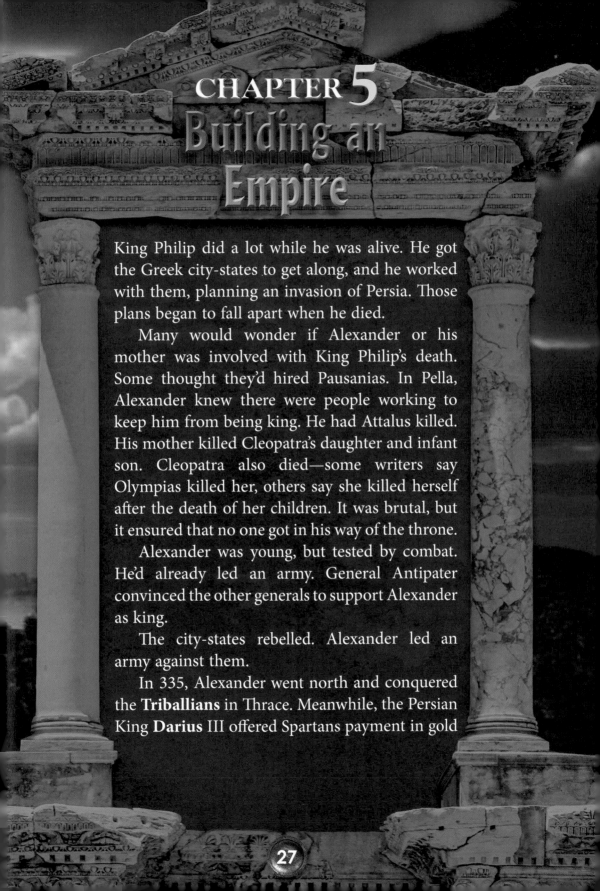

CHAPTER 5
Building an Empire

King Philip did a lot while he was alive. He got the Greek city-states to get along, and he worked with them, planning an invasion of Persia. Those plans began to fall apart when he died.

Many would wonder if Alexander or his mother was involved with King Philip's death. Some thought they'd hired Pausanias. In Pella, Alexander knew there were people working to keep him from being king. He had Attalus killed. His mother killed Cleopatra's daughter and infant son. Cleopatra also died—some writers say Olympias killed her, others say she killed herself after the death of her children. It was brutal, but it ensured that no one got in his way of the throne.

Alexander was young, but tested by combat. He'd already led an army. General Antipater convinced the other generals to support Alexander as king.

The city-states rebelled. Alexander led an army against them.

In 335, Alexander went north and conquered the **Triballians** in Thrace. Meanwhile, the Persian King **Darius** III offered Spartans payment in gold

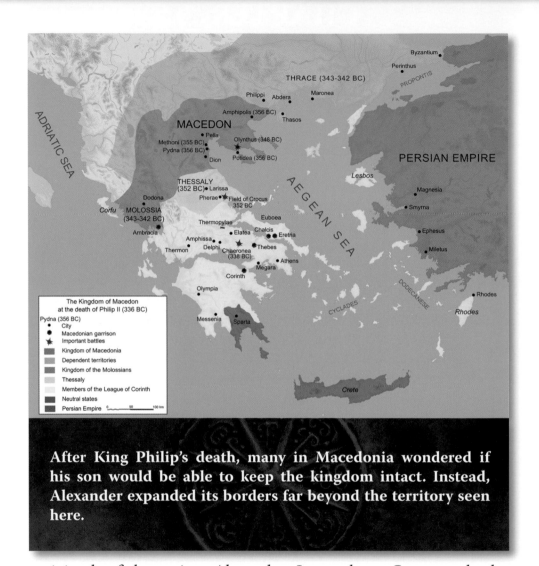

THRACE (343-342 BC)

MACEDON

PERSIAN EMPIRE

ADRIATIC SEA

AEGEAN SEA

THESSALY
(352 BC)

MOLOSSIA
(343-342 BC)

Field of Crocus
352 BC

Chaeronea
(338 BC)

The Kingdom of Macedon
at the death of Philip II (336 BC)

Pydna (356 BC)
● City
● Macedonian garrison
★ Important battles
█ Kingdom of Macedonia
█ Dependent territories
█ Kingdom of the Molossians
█ Thessaly
█ Members of the League of Corinth
█ Neutral states
█ Persian Empire

After King Philip's death, many in Macedonia wondered if his son would be able to keep the kingdom intact. Instead, Alexander expanded its borders far beyond the territory seen here.

to join the fight against Alexander. In southern Greece, a leader named **Demosthenes** claimed that Alexander had been killed in battle.

Believing the young king had died, the Thebans decided to declare their independence, and killed Macedonian soldiers. Alexander was enraged, and set out to prove to the Thebans that he was very much alive. Alexander and his army destroyed their town and killed thousands. They sold even more Thebans into slavery.

Alexander was not always merciful, but he could be just. Here, Timoclea is brought before him after she killed the man who attacked her. Alexander ordered her to be released.

The city-states agreed to rejoin the Corinthian League, led by Alexander. They gave him unlimited powers to attack Persia.

Although he had fewer soldiers, Alexander prepared to fight King Darius.

In the Spring of 334, Alexander's army crossed the **Hellespont**, the waterway between Greece and Asia. When he arrived on the other side, Alexander hurled a javelin. The spear sank deep into the sand as Alexander declared that the gods would soon give him Persia.

At the **Granicus** River (where Turkey is today) Alexander's forty thousand men met King Darius's even larger force. Alexander led thirteen cavalry squadrons through the river and met Darius's army on the other side. During the battle, his armor was pierced by a javelin. A hard blow landed across his helmet.

Alexander did not give up. He fought on with his cavalry beside him. The Macedonian phalanx crossed the river. Some of his enemy were Greek soldiers paid by King Darius. These men kept fighting even as the Persian army fled. Because of this, Alexander lost more men than he had in earlier battles. King Darius suffered far greater losses. Twenty thousand of his soldiers died.

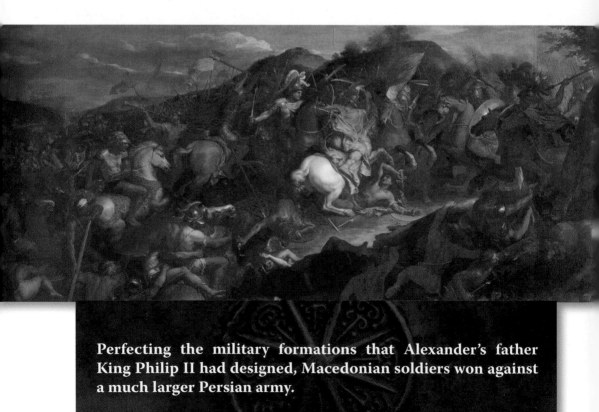

Perfecting the military formations that Alexander's father King Philip II had designed, Macedonian soldiers won against a much larger Persian army.

Alexander sent three hundred sets of Persian armor back to Greece. He wanted the Greeks to know that he deserved their support.

By June, Alexander's forces had taken over the Persian capital of **Sardes**. By the end of the summer, they had defeated the towns of **Miletus** and **Halicarnassus**.

He continued his conquests throughout Asia, arriving in the town of **Gordium** in 333 BCE. There, he was confronted with the famed **Gordian** knot. No one had been able to untie it. It was said that anyone who did would rule Asia.

Alexander approached the knot. He took a moment. A crowd circled him, waiting. "He saw the famous chariot fastened with cords made of the rind of the cornel-tree," Plutarch later wrote. ". . . Alexander finding himself unable to untie the knot, the ends of which were secretly twisted round and folded up within it, cut it asunder with his sword."[1]

He drew his sword and sliced the knot in two. Problem solved! It wasn't exactly untying it, but the people still celebrated. They believed Alexander was a god. He was starting to think so, too.

Alexander spent the summer in the town of Cilicia. To the north, Darius's army awaited. The forces met at **Issus** in November.

Although he was outnumbered, Alexander had a secret weapon (the **oblique** formation perfected by his father. Attacking only one side of the enemy's line, Alexander forced them to put more men on one side. When the rest of the line weakened, the remainder of Alexander's forces attacked.

Darius fled. He left behind not only soldiers and treasure, but his family. When Alexander invaded the royal camp, Darius was gone, but his wife, mother, and children remained. Other rulers might have killed them. Alexander commanded his men not to hurt them. Darius's mother bowed and thanked the tall warrior who'd saved her, not realizing that she was actually thanking Hephaestion. Alexander was not offended that she'd confused him with his best friend.

When Alexander's forces met the Persian Army at Issus the Macedonians overwhelmed them. King Darius fled, but Alexander spared the King's family.

But Alexander was not always so kind, as the soldiers of **Tyre** would soon learn.

While some cities were willing to accept Alexander's rule, Tyre didn't want to take sides until after the war between Darius and Alexander had ended. When Alexander requested to enter the city and worship in their temple, they refused him. Insulted, Alexander began a long siege. In order to reach their city, his men built a causeway—a raised roadway over the water. It was one-half mile long and made of stone. It was also well built, as it is still there today.

The Macedonian army mounted siege towers. Then they attacked.

The siege towers were moving platforms made of wood and covered in rawhide. Over 150 feet high, they had catapults on top— like large slingshots which launched stones at the Tyrians.

It took seven months for Alexander to defeat the town. As a warning to others who tried to slow him down, he had two thousand Tyrian soldiers crucified in addition to those already killed in battle.

In 332, Alexander entered Egypt. The Egyptians hated Darius's rule and welcomed the Greeks' arrival. In Egypt, Alexander planned a new city. Along the Mediterranean Sea, he selected an area which would make a good port. It would allow ships to load up with grain from Egypt and bring in goods from Europe. He wanted the city to be about art as well as money. Although the city he called Alexandria became famous as a center of culture, Alexander never saw his dream come true.

However, his dreams of defeating Darius did come true in 331. The final battle happened in the fall. It was fought in an area called **Gaugamela** or "camel's house." Alexander's forces were outnumbered. As nightfall arrived, he planned his attack. His generals tried to talk him into catching the large Persian force off guard by attacking at night. He refused.

All night, Darius's army stayed awake waiting for Alexander. When the sun rose, the men were very tired. Once again, Alexander's

After conquering Gaza, Alexander's next stop was Jerusalem. Here, he meets with the high priest in the Temple of Jerusalem.

forces used the oblique formation. Once again, it worked. The Persians fled. Thousands of them died but very few Macedonians were hurt. Unfortunately, King Darius had escaped again.

Alexander took over Darius's throne as ruler of Persia, but Darius was still alive. This created a dilemma for Alexander (if he managed to kill Darius, the Persian people would oppose him. But his position was not secure until Darius was out of the picture completely.

Bessus, one of Darius's generals, solved the problem. He killed Darius himself. After Macedonian soldiers arrested Bessus, Alexander had him executed. Persians hailed Alexander as a hero for capturing the killer of their king.

Alexander's army was ready for the war to be over. Their leader had captured Persia, and now they wanted to go home. But for Alexander, there were more lands to conquer.

Beginning in 329, his men fought the **Sogdians** in present-day **Tajikistan**. The Sogdians had built a fortress inside what was known as the Sogdian Rock. With steep cliffs on all sides, they believed no

This painting illustrates the founding of Alexandria, Egypt. Although the city would later become famous for literature and the arts, Alexander would not live to see Alexandria's success.

As Alexander and his army traveled through Persia, the desert proved to be a challenging environment. His men went without water for long periods of time. When a little water was found, it was offered to Alexander, but he refused because it was not enough to share with his men.

one could take their fortress. After fighting for two years, Alexander suggested that they surrender. They laughed, telling Alexander to find soldiers with wings. During the night, Alexander ordered some three hundred of his soldiers to climb the rock—scaling dangerous cliffs. When the Sogdians awoke to find Alexander's soldiers on top of the mountain, they surrendered immediately.

Not long after that victory, Alexander married a sixteen-year-old girl from Persia named Roxanne. He believed marrying her would create unity between Persia and Greece.

In 326, his forces faced one of their greatest challenges—not from men, but from elephants. Two hundred soldiers atop elephants formed a line along the River **Hydaspes**. This presented a problem

Alexander the Great added Babylon to his empire in 331 BCE. Because Alexander often lowered taxes and granted more freedom to the people under his rule, he was able to maintain control of a very large kingdom.

for Alexander's cavalry because their horses were afraid of elephants. But if Alexander won, he would defeat King **Porus** and rule India.

Alexander's men threw spears and shot arrows at the elephants' legs and at the soldiers on the elephants' backs. The animals stampeded—running fast and crushing Porus's army. Porus did not flee, but continue to fight until he was wounded.

Inspired by his bravery, Alexander allowed King Porus to remain in control of India, although it became part of the huge Macedonian empire. In that battle, however, his heart was broken when his beloved horse Bucephalus died. He would later found a city in his horse's honor. Many of his men, tired of fighting to conquer more and more lands, began asking to go home. After consulting with the gods, Alexander agreed. The soldiers who survived the journey back to Greece became very rich men as they were allowed to keep large amounts of gold and treasure from the battles.

Although Alexander had won dozens of battles, he could not recover from the loss of his best friend. After Hephaestion died in 324, Alexander was never quite the same.

The next year, he was planning more battles and more conquests when he fell ill. He suffered for more than a week before dying on either June 10 or 11, 323. He had spent over a decade fighting. He never returned to Greece or to his mother. Alexander's body was laid to rest in Alexandria, Egypt, the city he had helped plan.

Alexander's death is illustrated here in this painting by Karl von Piloty. After spending his entire adult life on a military campaign, Alexander died in Babylon, far from his home in Macedonia.

End of an Empire

No one person seemed able to manage the large empire Alexander had created. It wound up being divided between three of his generals (**Antigonus**, **Seleucus**, and Ptolemy. They fought each other for control of Alexander's lands in the Wars of the **Diadochi** which lasted until 281 BCE.

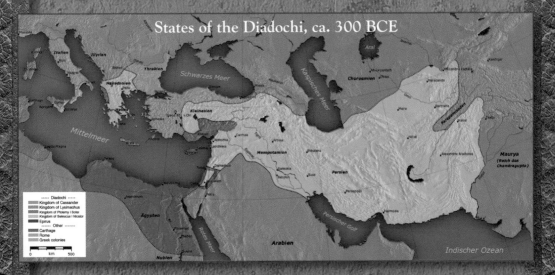

States of the Diadochi, ca. 300 BCE

When the war ended, the families of the generals each controlled a section of Alexander's kingdom. The family of Antigonus would run Macedonia and much of Greece. Seleucus was put in charge of Persia. Egypt was ruled by Ptolemy. Under his control, Alexandria became the capital of Egypt. It would become world famous as a place for both commerce and education. Many of the great minds of the time traveled to the Library of Alexandria.

In 146 BCE, Roman forces invaded Greece. All three regions would eventually come under Roman control.

Few suffered as much as Alexander's family. In the fifteen years or so after his death, his mother, wife, son, sister, and half-brother would all be killed in the battle for control of Alexander's empire.

BCE

356
Alexander is born in Macedonia to King Philip and his wife Olympias. His birthday is uncertain, but several sources report that it was on or around July 20.

ca. 350
Alone with Persian ambassadors, young Alexander impresses the Persians with his questions.

ca. 348–343
Alexander is taught math and military tactics by Leonidas.

ca. 344
Rides a horse no one else can. He names him Bucephalus.

343
Aristotle begins teaching Alexander philosophy, medicine, and the arts.

340
Alexander's formal schooling ends, and he begins joining his father on military raids. After his father appoints him Regent of Macedonia, Alexander puts down a revolt and founds Alexandropolis.

338
Macedonian Army defeats Athens and Thebes. King Phailip establishes the Corinthian League.

336
After King Philip is killed, Alexander is made king of Macedonia.

335
Alexander leads an attack on Thebes, destroying the city after a revolt.

334
Conquest of Asia Minor begins.

333
Defeats Persia's King Darius III at the Battle of Issus.

ca. 332
Founds Alexandria in Egypt.

331
Alexander wins the Battle of Gaugamela against the Persian forces even though his army is outnumbered.

330
After King Darius is killed, Alexander becomes the Great King of Persia.

327
Alexander and his army invade India.

| 326 | In the Battle of the Hydaspes, India is added to the Macedonian Empire, but his horse Bucephalus dies in battle. The next year, he founds a city in the horse's honor. He calls it Bucephala. |
| 323 | On June 10 or 11, Alexander dies from illness. |

The Funeral Procession of Alexander the Great by André Bauchant

TIMELINE

BCE

776	The first Olympic Games are held.
ca. 700	Homer writes the *Iliad* and *Odyssey* poems. Alexander will later identify with Achilles, the hero of the *Iliad*.
ca. 550	In Athens, male citizens are allowed to vote on how the city is run. Women and non-citizens are not allowed to vote.

490	King Darius I and his army of twenty-five thousand Persians are defeated by ten thousand Greeks in the Battle of Marathon (which later gives its name to the twenty-six-mile race).
ca. 480	The Golden Age of Greece begins.
480	When a huge Persian army tries to invade Greece, the largely outnumbered Greeks defend their territory for three days before retreating. Later that year, a huge sea battle takes place between Persians and Greeks near Athens and the island of Salamis. The Greeks win that battle.
479	Greeks defeat the Persian Army at the Battle of Plataea. This battle ends the Persian invasion.
431	The Peloponnesian War begins between Athens and Sparta.
404	Athens surrenders to Sparta. Spartans limit democracy in Athens.
403	Democracy is restored in Athens.
399	Accused of negatively influencing youth and not believing in the gods of Athens, philosopher Socrates is tried and executed.
ca. 387	The Academy is opened by Plato in Athens.
359	Philip II becomes King of Macedonia.
ca. 335	Aristotle founds the Lyceum, a school in Athens.
322	Aristotle dies. Wars of the Diadochi begin to be fought for control of Alexander's territory.
301	Lysimachus and Seleucus defeat Antigonus at the Battle of Ipsus.
281	Wars of the Diadochi end, resulting in four kingdoms (the Ptolemaic Kingdom, the Seleucid Kingdom, the Antigonid Kingdom, and the Attalid Kingdom.
30	Cleopatra, the last pharaoh of the Ptolemaic Kingdom in Egypt, dies.

Chapter 1. A Bold Boy
1. Plutarch, *The Life of Alexander*, translated by John Dryden. http://classics.mit.edu/Plutarch/alexandr.html

Chapter 2. A Horse is a Horse
1. Plutarch, *The Life of Alexander*, translated by Bernadotte Perrin. http://penelope.uchicago.edu/Thayer/E/Roman/Texts/Plutarch/Lives/Alexander*/home.html
2. Plutarch, *The Life of Alexander*, translated by John Dryden. http://classics.mit.edu/Plutarch/alexandr.html
3. Ibid.
4. Ibid.

Chapter 3. School of Hard Knocks
1. Plutarch, *The Life of Alexander*, translated by John Dryden. http://classics.mit.edu/Plutarch/alexandr.html
2. Ibid.

Chapter 4. Studying to Rule
1. Plutarch, *The Life of Alexander*, translated by John Dryden. http://classics.mit.edu/Plutarch/alexandr.html
2. Fox, Robin Lane. *Alexander the Great.* New York (Penguin, 1973. p. 54.
3. Plutarch, *The Life of Alexander*, translated by John Dryden. http://classics.mit.edu/Plutarch/alexandr.html
4. Ibid.
5. Ibid.

Chapter 5. Building an Empire
1. Plutarch, *The Life of Alexander*, translated by John Dryden. http://classics.mit.edu/Plutarch/alexandr.html

Books

Bankston, John. *The Life and Times of Alexander the Great.* Hockessin, DE (Mitchell Lane Publishers, 2005.

Demi. *Alexander the Great.* New York (Marshall Cavendish Children, 2010.

Lasker, Joe. *The Great Alexander the Great.* New York (Viking Press, 1983.

Marsico, Katie. *Alexander the Great (Ancient King & Conqueror.* Edina, MN (ABDO Pub. Co., 2009.

Pearson, Anne. *Ancient Greece.* New York (DK Pub., 2004.

Rice, Rob S. *Ancient Greek Warfare.* Pleasantville, NY (GS Learning Library, 2010.

Shecter, Vicky. *Alexander the Great Rocks the World.* Plain City, OH (Darby Creek Pub., 2006.

Shone, Rob, and Anita Ganeri. A*lexander the Great (The Life of a King and Conqueror.* New York (Rosen Central, 2005.

On the Internet

"Alexander the Great." National Geographic Channel Video. http://channel.nationalgeographic.com/channel/videos/alexander-the-great/

"Ancient Greeks (The Greek World." BBC Primary History. http://www.bbc.co.uk/schools/primaryhistory/ancient_greeks/greek_world/

Barrow, Mandy. "Interactive Greece." Ancient Greece. http://www.chiddingstone.kent.sch.uk/homework/greece/interactive.htm

Works Consulted

Cantor, Norman F. *Alexander the Great (Journey to the End of the Earth.* New York (HarperCollins Publishers, 2005.

Cartledge, Paul. "Alexander the Great (Hunting for a New Past." BBC History, February 17, 2011. http://www.bbc.co.uk/history/ancient/greeks/alexander_the_great_01.shtml

Fildes, Alan, and Joann Fletcher. *Alexander the Great (Son of the Gods.* Los Angeles (Getty Publications, 2002.

Fox, Robin Lane. *Alexander the Great.* New York (Penguin Books, 1973.

Freeman, Philip. *Alexander the Great.* New York (Simon & Schuster, 2011.

Grainger, John D. *Alexander the Great Failure (The Collapse of the Macedonian Empire.* London (Hambledon Continuum, 2007.

"Greece Timeline." Ancient-Greece.org. http://www.ancient-greece.org/resources/timeline.html

In the Footsteps of Alexander the Great. DVD. Directed by Michael Wood. BBC Worldwide, 1998.

Plutarch. *The Life of Alexander.* Translated by Bernadotte Perrin. http://penelope.uchicago.edu/Thayer/E/Roman/Texts/Plutarch/Lives/Alexander*/home.html

Plutarch. *The Life of Alexander.* Translated by John Dryden. http://classics.mit.edu/Plutarch/alexandr.html

Untereker, Jed, James Kossuth, and Bill Kelsey. "Alexander the Great," 1996. http://wso.williams.edu/~junterek/

PHONETIC PRONUNCIATIONS

Achilles (uh-KIL-eez)
Afghanistan (af-GAN-uh-stan)
Antigonus (an-TIG-uh-nuhs)
Antipater (an-TIP-uh-ter)
Aphrodite (af-ruh-DAHY-tee)
Aristotle (AR-uh-stot-l)
Attalus (AT-l-uhs)
Babylon (BAB-uh-luhn)
Bessus (BESS-uhs)
Bucephalus (byoo-SEF-uh-luhs)
Cassander (kuh-SAN-der)
Castaigne (kas-TAYN)
Chaeronea (ker-uh-NEE-uh)
Cleopatra (klee-uh-PA-truh)
Darius (duh-RAHY-uhs)
Demaratus (deh-mahr-AT-uhs)
Demosthenes
    (dih-MOS-thuh-neez)
Diadochi (dahy-ADD-uh-kee)
Diogenes (dahy-OJ-uh-neez)
Dionysus (dahy-uh-NAHY-suhs)
Epirus (ih-PAHY-ruhs)
Gaugamela (gaw-guh-MEE-luh)
Giovanni Battista Tiepolo (joh-
    VAH-nee buh-TEE-stuh
    tee-EP-uh-loh)
Granicus (gruh-NAHY-kuhs)
Gordian (GAWR-dee-uhn)
Gordium (GAWR-dee-uhm)
Guibal (GEE-buhl)
Halicarnassus
    (hal-uh-kahr-NAS-uhs)
Hellespont (HEL-uh-spont)
Hephaestion (he-FEES-tee-ahn)
Hydaspes (hahy-DAHS-pees)

Iliad (IL-ee-uhd)
Illyria (ih-LEER-ee-uh)
Issus (IS-uhs)
Leonidas (lee-ON-i-duhs)
Lysimachus (lahy-SIM-uh-kuhs)
Macedonia (mas-ih-DOH-nee-uh)
Maedi (MAHY-dee)
Mediterranean
    (med-ih-tuh-REY-nee-uhn)
Mieza (mee-AY-zuh)
Miletus (mahy-LEE-tuhs)
oblique (uh-BLEEK)
Olympias (uh-LIM-pee-uhs)
Pausanias (paw-SEY-nee-uhs)
Perikles (or Pericles) (PER-i-kleez)
Persia (PUR-zhuh)
Plato (PLEY-toh)
Plutarch (PLOO-tahrk)
Porus (PUHW-ruhs)
Ptolemy (TOL-uh-mee)
Sardes (SAHR-dis)
sarissa (sahr-IH-suh)
Schönbrunn (shen-BRUNN)
Seleucus (si-LOO-kuhs)
Sinope (suh-NOH-pee)
Socrates (SOK-ruh-teez)
Socratic (soh-KRAT-ik)
Sogdian (SOG-dee-uhn)
Styx (STIKS)
Tajikistan (tuh-JIK-uh-stan)
Timoclea (tih-MOK-leh-uh)
Triballian (trih-BALL-yuhn)
Tyre (TAHY-uhr)
Zeus (ZOOS)

PHOTO CREDITS (Cover, pp. 1, 35—Placido Costanzi; pp. 4, 11, 14, 18, 20—Photos. com; p. 6—Giovanni Battista Tiepolo; p. 8—François Schommer; pp. 12, 17, 23, 25, 28, 30, 39—cc-by-sa; p. 26—Andre Castainge; p. 29—Domenico Zampieri; p. 32—Albrecht Altdorfer; p. 34—Sebastiano Conca; p. 36—Giuseppe Cades; p. 37—Charles Le Brun; p. 38—Karl von Piloty; p. 41—André Bauchant. Every effort has been made to locate all copyright holders of materials used in this book. Any errors or omissions will be corrected in future editions of the book.

Causeway (KAWZ-way)—A raised road made of stone or concrete built across water or wet land.

Cavalry (KAV-al-ree)—A section of an army made up of soldiers fighting on horseback.

City-state—An independent area of ancient Greece that was self-ruled.

Crucify (KRU-suh-fahy)—Brutal means of putting criminals to death by nailing their hands and feet to a raised cross of wood.

Democracy (deh-MOK-ruh-see)—A government in which the control belongs to the people.

Execution (ek-suh-KYU-shun)—Death as punishment for a crime.

Infantry (IN-fuhn-tree)—Soldiers who fight on foot with the most simple weapons.

Javelin (JAV-uh-lin)—A very light throwing spear.

Phalanx (FAY-langks)—Soldiers who fight together as an organized group.

Revolt (ri-VOHLT)—Uprising or rebellion against those in power.

Siege (SEEJ)—The surrounding of an area in order to force the people to surrender.

Stampede (stam-PEED)—Fast and wild rush in one direction, usually by animals.